Making a New Nation

WESTWARD TO THE PACIFIC

From the Trail of Tears to the Transcontinental Railroad

Ted Schaefer

HEINEMANN LIBRARY
CHICAGO, ILLINOIS

Designed by Philippa Baile and Kim Miracle
Maps by Jeff Edwards
Printed and bound in China by WKT Company Limited

11 10 09 08 07
10 9 8 7 6 5 4 3 2 1

Library of Congress Cataloging-in-Publication Data
Schaefer, Ted, 1948-
 Westward to the Pacific / Ted Schaefer.
    p. cm. -- (Making a new nation)
 Includes bibliographical references and index.
 ISBN 1-4034-7829-5 (library binding-hardcover) -- ISBN 1-4034-7836-8 (pbk.)
 1. United States--Territorial expansion--History--Juvenile literature. 2. West (U.S.)-
-History--Juvenile literature. 3. Frontier and pioneer life--West (U.S.)--Juvenile
literature. 4. United States--Historical geography--Juvenile literature. I. Title. II. Series.
E179.5.S32 2006
 911'.73--dc22

                                    2006003250

Acknowledgments
The author and publisher are grateful to the following for permission to reproduce
copyright material: Alamy Images/Westend61 p. **43**; Art Resource, NY/Smithsonian
American Art Museum, Washington, DC p. **17**; Art Resource, NY/The New York Public
Library pp. **36**, **39**; Bridgeman Art Library/Private Collection, Peter Newark American
Pictures p. **20**; Corbis pp. **34** (David Muench), **19**, **33**, **40**; Corbis/Bettmann pp. **14**, **26**,
31, **41**; Corbis/Burstein Collection p. **5**; Corbis/Joseph Sohm, ChromoSohm Inc p. **15**;
Denver Public Library, Western History Collection, X-11929 p. **37**; Getty Images p. **32**
(Bob Thomason); Getty Images/Altrendo p. **24**; Harcourt Education Ltd p. **35**; Library
of Congress pp. **13**, **29**; Lonely Planet Images p. **25** (Richard Cummins); Northwind
Picture Archives pp. **8**, **11**, **12**, **16**, **18**, **23**; The Granger Collection, New York pp. **6**,
10, **27**, **38**, **42**.

Cover photograph reproduced with the permission of N Currier/Getty Images.

The publishers would like to thank Kathryn Burns-Howard for her help in the
preparation of this book.

Every effort has been made to contact copyright holders of any material reproduced in
this book. Any omissions will be rectified in subsequent printings if notice is given to
the publisher.

CONTENTS

Some words are shown in bold, **like this**. You can find
out what they mean by looking in the glossary.

A NATION ON THE MOVE

In 1800 the young country called the United States of America seemed to be bursting with promise. The nation had a new kind of government that was formed by the people, for the people. The population was healthy, **prosperous**, and growing.

At this time, the United States consisted of sixteen states: the original thirteen **colonies**, plus Vermont, Kentucky, and Tennessee. The country also included **territory** that reached west to the Mississippi River and north to the Great Lakes. Ohio became the seventeenth state in 1803. That same year, the Louisiana Purchase doubled the size of the country. This rich land stretched far beyond the Mississippi River.

The United States was a new country in a New World. The American people were learning to govern themselves and solve their own problems. Around the world, Americans were becoming known for their ideas.

This map shows the United States in 1804.

WHERE PEOPLE LIVED

At this time, 95 percent of Americans lived on farms. The other five percent lived in cities. Farmers owned their land and grew crops to eat and to sell. Most people who lived in the cities were traders and merchants who ran small businesses.

The Allegheny Mountains, which run through present-day West Virginia, Virginia, Maryland, and Pennsylvania, had once been considered a **barrier** to **settlement**. By 1804, however, four million Americans lived on the west side of the mountains. This was more people than lived on the east side.

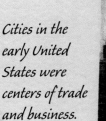

Cities in the early United States were centers of trade and business.

Rivers and canals

In the early 1800s, rivers were the best form of transportation. The few roads that existed were rough and could not carry heavy loads. **Settlers** built their homes near rivers for easy access to transportation. At one time, one-fourth of the nation's population lived along the Ohio River. The rivers people used were not always connected to each other. Canals were dug to join rivers and lakes together, so new places could be reached. People and goods traveled these waterways until the 1830s, when steamboats and railroads became the main methods of transportation.

EXPANDING THE FRONTIER

After the Louisiana Purchase was completed, President Thomas Jefferson sent an **expedition** to explore and map the new territory. Meriwether Lewis and William Clark led this expedition. When Jefferson realized how much land there was in the Louisiana Purchase, he thought it would take 100 generations of Americans to settle it all. In reality, it would only take four.

The wild lands that lay beyond the settled areas were called the **frontier**. In the beginning, when people first settled in North America, the frontier started only a few miles from the shore of the Atlantic Ocean. The fast-growing population quickly pushed it to the west.

Sacajawea was a Shoshone woman who guided Lewis and Clark on their expedition.

A great man

Thomas Jefferson joined the fight that won **independence** for the United States. He was the author of the Declaration of Independence. In 1801 he became the third president of the United States. Jefferson was the first westward-thinking president. In his first speech after being elected, he called the United States "a rising nation, spread over a wide and fruitful land."

OPENING THE WEST

By 1820 Americans had settled as far west as the Mississippi River. The frontier then was the unknown land across the river. It would not remain unknown for much longer.

Lewis and Clark showed the way. Their glowing descriptions of the new land aroused great interest in the cities in the eastern United States. Maps and journals from their expedition showed trails, rivers, and mountain passes. Other **explorers** used this information and added their own discoveries. The great empty lands to the west were opened.

MIGRATION

The pull of opportunity in the West combined with the push of a restless, swelling population in the East. This created a mass **migration** across the United States. Waves of settlers moved westward across the country, searching for a better way of life.

The West, however, was not empty. There were millions of Native Americans living there, as they had been for thousands of years. The arrival of settlers meant death for many Native Americans.

This map shows where different Native Americans lived in North America around 1800.

FIGHTING FOR LAND

When **colonists** first made contact with Native Americans, many **tribes** were friendly. Some Native Americans welcomed settlers and helped them learn how to get food and live in their new land. Many people would have starved and early settlements would have failed without help from Native Americans.

The white settlers, however, felt that Native Americans did not have a right to the land. Settlers felt they could put the land to better use and that it was their right to settle the land. Thousands of settlers swarmed into the **Northwest Territory**. Native Americans became fearful that they would not be able to continue living in their homelands. Some began to fight back.

Some Native Americans fought against new settlers.

Squatters

The first settlers were squatters. That means they moved onto land that they did not own. The government told people not to settle on Native American land, but some did anyway. Then, when Native Americans fought against the settlers, the settlers pressured the government to protect them from the Native Americans.

TROUBLE WITH ENGLAND

Native Americans had an **ally** in their fight. The British gave them guns and encouraged them to resist the settlers. Ever since the American colonies had rebelled against British rule, Great Britain and the United States had disagreed over **borders**.

The United States had other problems with Great Britain. The British had been stopping U.S. merchant ships and seizing **cargo**. U.S. sailors were kidnapped and forced to work for the British. From 1803 to 1812, several thousand U.S. sailors were forced to work for the British Navy.

THE WAR OF 1812

The American people became angry. Some wanted war with the British, so that they could drive the British out of North America. These people, called "war hawks," voted for candidates for **Congress** who felt the same way. In June of 1812, Congress declared war on England. It was the beginning of a war that would last for three years.

The National Road

The National Road was the first road built by the U.S. government. Construction began in 1811 in Cumberland, Maryland. The road was completed to the Ohio River by 1818 and eventually reached Vandalia, Illinois, in the 1830s.

The National Road helped Americans reach the Midwest and start new settlements there.

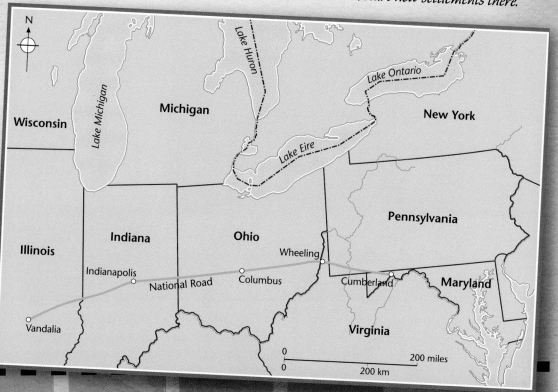

FIGHTING ON LAND AND WATER

During the War of 1812, British and U.S. forces fought many battles on and around the Great Lakes. Some Native American **tribes**, such as the Shawnee and the Delaware, fought on the side of the British. A Native American leader named Tecumseh united these tribes. Tecumseh later became a general in the British Army. He thought the war was the last chance for Native Americans to save their land.

Tecumseh, a Shawnee, united Native Americans in battle against the settlers.

The words of Tecumseh

Tecumseh took his message to Native American tribes to inspire them to fight against the settlers. He said, "Let the white race perish! They seize your land, they corrupt your women, they trample on the bones of your dead. Back whence they came, upon a trail of blood, they must be driven. Burn their houses, destroy their stock! The red man owns the country and the palefaces must never enjoy it. War now, war forever!"

MORE BATTLES

In 1813 the British and their Native American allies were defeated at the Battle of the Thames in southern Canada. Tecumseh was killed. This battle marked the end of conflict in the Northwest Territory between Native Americans and white settlers.

The war went on. In 1814 British troops captured Washington, D.C., and burned down the White House. Then, they attacked Baltimore, but they could not defeat the Americans at **Fort** McHenry. The war ended when Great Britain and the United States signed the **Treaty** of Ghent on December 24, 1814.

Two weeks later, news of the peace treaty had still not reached New Orleans. It was January 1815, and British ships carrying 7,500 troops attacked the city. The U.S. defenders, led by General Andrew Jackson, won a great victory. Jackson became a national hero.

The tribes that fought on the side of the British were punished after the war. The U.S. government made them sign new treaties that forced the Native Americans to give up large areas of land. Waves of new settlers moved in.

In this battle scene from the War of 1812, the USS Constitution sinks the British HMS Guerriere.

THE AGE OF JACKSON

Andrew Jackson was already famous as a fighter when he became a national hero at the Battle of New Orleans. In March 1814 General Jackson had led a force that included "White Stick" Creek Native Americans against "Red Stick" Creeks who had sided with the British.

The Red Sticks were defeated at the Battle of Horseshoe Bend. The treaty that resulted was a disaster for all of the Creeks. The White Sticks lost most of their land and the Red Sticks lost all of theirs.

Jackson grew up fighting against Native Americans..

FORCED TREATIES

After the War of 1812, Andrew Jackson was appointed to be in charge of making treaties with Native Americans. When tribes were defeated in battle, they had to sign treaties to end the fighting. In these agreements, tribes gave up large parts of their land. Between 1815 and 1820, the government seized territory that became parts of present-day Florida, Georgia, North Carolina, Mississippi, and Kentucky.

THE ERA OF GOOD FEELINGS

The period following the War of 1812 became known as the Era of Good Feelings. Americans were proud that the United States had stood up to a major world power. The British had to give up some territories in the North. In 1819 the U.S. government bought the parts of Florida that it did not yet own from Spain. The United States had secure borders, more territory, and respect in the world. People had new confidence in the future of the country.

The Monroe Doctrine

In 1823, President James Monroe gave a speech in which he acknowledged other countries' existing colonies. However, he warned the European nations against attempting to expand their colonies in North America. This was known as the Monroe Doctrine. It became permanent government **policy**.

President Monroe wanted to stop Spain, Russia, and France from expanding their colonies or starting new ones.

PRESIDENT JACKSON

In 1828 Andrew Jackson ran for president as a "man of the people." All six of the presidents up until then had come from wealthy, educated families. Jackson was different. He had been born to a poor family in a log cabin. By the age of fourteen, he was an **orphan** and had to raise and educate himself.

Jackson believed that Native Americans were dangerous and a threat to white settlements. He wanted to push out all Native Americans living east of the Mississippi River. Jackson became very popular and was elected the seventh president of the United States.

In 1830 he promoted and signed the Indian Removal Act. This law stated that all Native Americans living in the East had to leave their lands and move to the West, across the Mississippi River. The U.S. Army would force out those who would not leave willingly.

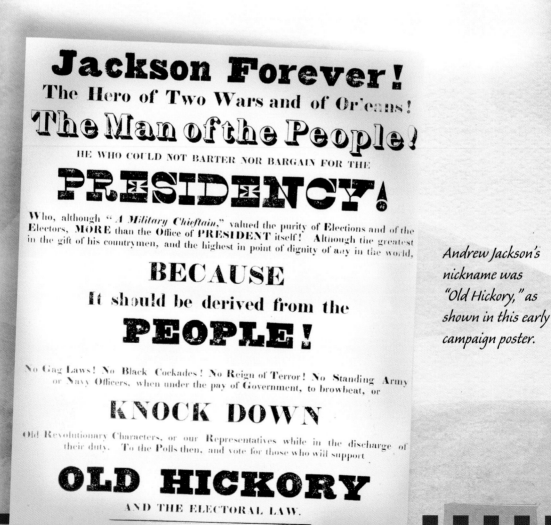

Andrew Jackson's nickname was "Old Hickory," as shown in this early campaign poster.

A STRONGER COUNTRY

President Andrew Jackson made the United States stronger, but he did so at the expense of Native Americans. Jackson showed that anyone could become president and that the government really did represent the people. During his time as president, ordinary citizens became more involved in politics and government. The United States was the most democratic country in the world at that time, and it grew even more united. The Native Americans, however, paid a terrible price for the prosperity felt by the rest of the country.

*The **Constitution** is the most important document in U.S. democracy.*

The downside of democracy

In a **democracy**, the people make the rules. They are free to make choices about their lives and government. When many people have unjust ideas, democracies can be unfair and commit evil acts. The treatment of the Native Americans by the U.S. government is a good example. The government reflected the will of the people, but some people had **racist** attitudes and selfish motives. The good side of democracy is that people can learn from previous mistakes and change their government to make it better.

TRAIL OF TEARS

Native Americans who lived between the Atlantic Ocean and the Mississippi River were Eastern Woodlands Native Americans. For hundreds of years, they had inhabited the vast forests that covered the land before European colonists arrived. The lifestyle of a tribe depended on where they lived. Most were skilled hunters who stalked wild animals for food. They knew how to find other foods like nuts, berries, and plants. In some areas, they fished and farmed.

The first white settlements were along the Atlantic coast. As the population grew, all the best land near the coast was taken. New settlers had to travel farther west, into lands that belonged to the Native Americans.

White settlers moved into areas that appeared to be unoccupied. They cut down the trees and killed the buffalo and other animals. They built homes and farms and villages. The land they built on, however, was already occupied. It was the hunting grounds that Native Americans depended on for food.

Native Americas used materials from the land and animals to build their homes.

FIGHTING BACK

Some Native Americans fought to save their homelands. The strongest resistance came from tribes that had been united by the Shawnee leader Tecumseh. Tribes worked together to fight against the settlers and the U.S. Army. But in 1811, the army attacked the Shawnee camp on the Tippecanoe River. The Native Americans were defeated and their resistance was crushed.

Tecumseh was not at the camp when it was destroyed. He was traveling in the South, trying to convince other tribes to unite. One of those tribes was the Seminoles, who lived in Florida.

Osceola became a courageous leader of his people.

The story of Osceola
Among the Seminoles who listened to Tecumseh's message was a young boy named Osceola. He heard the fighting words and kept them in his heart. He led the Seminole people in a strong defense of their homeland in the swamps and forests of Florida. Many armies were sent against them, but Osceola and his warriors defeated them all. Finally, the army tricked Osceola and captured him. He was put in prison and died of disease.

FIVE TRIBES

Some Native Americans began to adapt to new ways of living. They lived like the settlers and became farmers and raised livestock instead of hunting. In the southeastern United States, some tribes began to adopt so much of the white lifestyle that they became known as the Five Civilized Tribes. These were the Creek, Chickasaw, Choctaw, Seminole, and the largest of the five, the Cherokee.

Cherokee Alphabet.

Sequoyah and the syllabary

Sequoyah was a Cherokee tribal leader. He saw that knowing how to read and write allowed white men to exchange ideas without meeting. None of the Native American tribes had a written language, but Sequoyah was determined to create one for the Cherokee. It was called a syllabary because each of the 85 symbols or letters stands for a **syllable** of the Cherokee language. Thousands of people quickly learned to read and write using Sequoyah's syllabary. Soon there were books and newspapers printed in the Cherokee language.

It took Sequoyah twelve years to develop the Cherokee syllabary.

THE CHEROKEE NATION

Most Cherokee wanted to live peacefully with their white neighbors. They became farmers and traders instead of hunters and warriors. They lived in permanent homes made of boards and bricks. Cherokee farms and **plantations** grew crops, including cotton. Some Cherokee even had African **slaves**, just like the white people.

The Cherokee Nation adopted a constitution and had an elected **governor**. They started a system of courts to enforce Cherokee laws. Their capital had government buildings, schools, churches, and businesses. A network of roads connected villages into a nation that looked much like the white nation that bordered it.

But Native Americans and whites looked at land much differently. To the Native Americans, land was the source of life. It gave them food and materials for their clothing and homes. They believed their homelands were sacred (holy) and belonged to the whole tribe. To white settlers, land was a source of personal wealth and comfort. They thought individuals should own land, including the land where Native Americans lived.

Anti-Native American information exaggerated attacks on white settlers.

TAKING NATIVE AMERICAN LAND

A pattern of events developed that was repeated again and again across the country. Settlers moved onto Native American land. Some Native Americans used force to resist the white settlers. The Native Americans were blamed for violence, and the settlers demanded protection. Then, the government sent soldiers to fight against the Native Americans. Finally, a treaty would be arranged to end the fighting.

The Cherokee were pushed into a smaller and smaller area. They tried every way they could to save their nation. Their leaders pleaded with the government to keep its promises. But the government carried out the wishes of the whites, who wanted all Native Americans removed.

The Cherokee issued a formal protest to the U.S. government.

Broken promises

People knew it was not right to just take Native American land. Treaties were made between the government and Native American tribes to make white ownership of land seem legal. Between 1789 and 1835, the U.S. government signed dozens of treaties with the Cherokee. With each treaty, the Native Americans had to surrender more land, but were promised that this time they would be secure within their new borders. White settlers violated every treaty that was made.

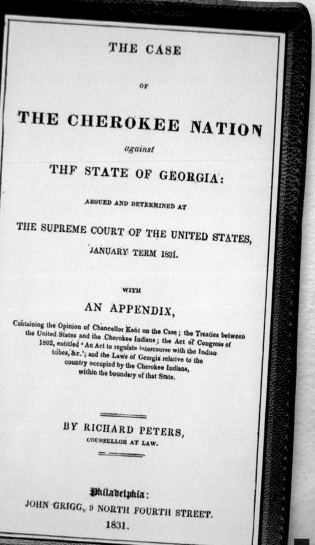

THE CASE

OF

THE CHEROKEE NATION

against

THE STATE OF GEORGIA:

ARGUED AND DETERMINED AT

THE SUPREME COURT OF THE UNITED STATES,

JANUARY TERM 1831.

WITH

AN APPENDIX,

Containing the Opinion of Chancellor Kent on the Case ; the Treaties between the United States and the Cherokee Indians ; the Act of Congress of 1802, entitled ' An Act to regulate intercourse with the Indian tribes, &c.'; and the Laws of Georgia relative to the country occupied by the Cherokee Indians, within the boundary of that State.

BY RICHARD PETERS,
COUNSELLOR AT LAW.

Philadelphia:
JOHN GRIGG, 9 NORTH FOURTH STREET.
1831.

FORCED OUT

By 1838 most of the Cherokee had died or moved to the West. About 16,000 were left in the East, mostly living in Georgia. They refused to leave because they knew they were right. The government bowed to the will of the settlers and sent the army to remove the last Native Americans. The Cherokee were forcibly removed from their homes and made to move west to Oklahoma Territory.

It was a harsh journey. They were forced to go without enough food or clothing, and soon it was winter. Most had to walk. Diseases were easily passed around. Every night people died from sickness and cold. Every morning the dead were buried and the survivors marched on.

The Cherokee were heartbroken. Their homeland was gone and the graves of thousands of their people marked the **routes** of their journey west. It became known as the Trail of Tears.

Several different trails formed the Trail of Tears.

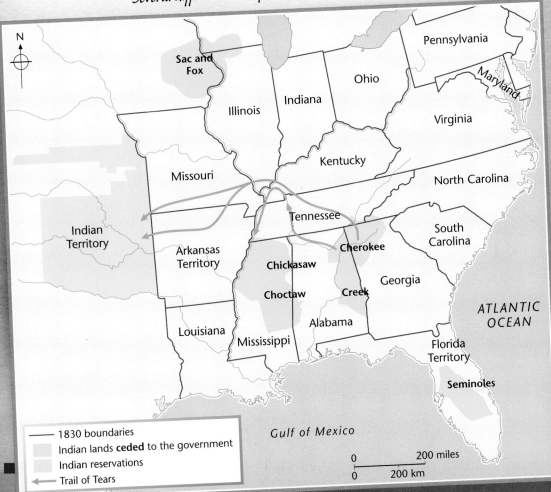

- —— 1830 boundaries
- Indian lands **ceded** to the government
- Indian reservations
- ← Trail of Tears

IMMIGRANTS AND PIONEERS

A migrant is a person who moves from place to place. An **immigrant** is a person who comes from one country to live in another. Most of the people who settled the West had previously lived in the eastern United States. They migrated to western lands to start new lives. Many other settlers had come from much farther away. They came from Great Britain, Ireland, Germany, and other European countries. People also came from China, Australia, and South America.

Fresh air, pure water, and rich soil made the United States an attractive place to live. The death rate was low and the birth rate was twice as high as in Europe. Many families had lots of children, and the population increased rapidly, spreading from east to west.

A nation's center of population is the place where there are an equal number of people living to the north, south, east, and west. It changes over the years.

Immigrants and population

Year	U.S. Population	Immigrants in Last Ten Years
1830	12.8 million	151,824
1840	17 million	599,000
1850	23.1 million	1.7 million
1860	31.4 million	2.6 million

PIONEERS

The **pioneers** were the first people to settle in a new place. The greatest single motivation for settling on the frontier was the chance to own land. This was especially true for those who came from Europe, where only royalty and the very rich were landowners. Many people migrated to the West to escape racial or religious **discrimination**. These motivations came to be called the American Dream: a chance for freedom, wealth, and a better life.

Making a new home

As difficult as the journey was, the hard work was just starting when the settlers finally reached their new land. They had to cut down trees, build a house, find a source of water, and clear land to plant crops. Pioneers had to be independent and make things for themselves. There were no stores, tailors, or shoemakers. People had to grow their own food and make their own clothes.

Settlers needed to clear many trees before they could plant their fields.

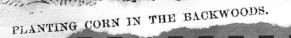

PLANTING CORN IN THE BACKWOODS.

REMEMBER THE ALAMO

The first U.S. settlers reached Texas in 1821, when it was still a part of Mexico. It was a land of many **natural resources**, with rivers, forests, rich soil for farming, and grassy plains. Texas covered a large area, but few people lived there.

Native Americans had lived in Texas for hundreds of years. About 4,000 Tejanos, or Mexican settlers, lived there, too. The Native Americans and the Tejanos did not get along and sometimes fought with each other.

The Mexican government wanted more white people to settle in Texas so it would grow and become stronger. They invited U.S. settlers to move there and offered them land for a cheap price. Stephen Austin led the first group of about 300 families. They started a settlement near the Brazos River. Within ten years, thousands of Americans had moved to Texas.

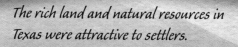

The rich land and natural resources in Texas were attractive to settlers.

REVOLT AGAINST MEXICO

At first, Americans were happy to live under Mexican rule. Eventually, however, the Mexican government decided that too many people were coming from the United States. Laws were passed that banned new immigrants, raised taxes, and took away the rights of the settlers. Mexican soldiers were sent to Texas to enforce the laws.

The people of Texas became angry and revolted against Mexico. They wanted to become independent. Volunteers drove the Mexican soldiers out of San Antonio, took over an old **mission** there, and made it into a fort. It was called the Alamo.

General Santa Anna, the Mexican president, vowed to crush the revolution. He led his army into Texas. On February 23, 1836, 6,000 Mexican soldiers surrounded the Alamo. Inside were fewer than 200 defenders.

Defenders of the Alamo

The volunteers at the Alamo included Americans and Tejanos. Two legendary frontiersmen, Davy Crockett and James Bowie, joined them in their fight for freedom. Colonel William Travis led the force. He sent out a letter to all Americans. Part of his letter said, "I shall never surrender or retreat. Victory or death!"

These statues honoring the memory of the defenders of the Alamo are located in San Antonio, Texas.

C. KIMBLE · WILLIAM P. KING · JOHN G. KING · WILLIAM IRVINE LEWIS
IEL MELTON · THOMAS R. MILLER · WILLIAM MILLS · ISAAC MI
ISTOPHER A. PARKER · JUAN ANTONIO PADILLO · WILLIAM PA
H. SMITH · CHARLES S. SMITH · JOSHUA G. SMITH · WI
N · BURKE TRAMMEL · WILLIAM BARRET TRA

BATTLE OF THE ALAMO

The Mexican Army fired cannons at the Alamo. Soldiers attacked with swords and guns. The Texans inside shot back, killing and wounding many Mexicans. For twelve days, Santa Anna's soldiers continued their attack. Cannons fired again and again at the thick walls of the old mission.

On the thirteenth day, Santa Anna ordered his men to charge the fort. The Mexicans attacked from every direction, shouting and firing their guns. Hundreds of soldiers climbed the walls. The Texan settlers fought bravely. The fighting was fast and hard. But there were too many soldiers. All the defenders were killed. Santa Anna's army won the Battle of the Alamo.

For the first twelve days of the attack at the Alamo, Colonel Travis fired his own cannon so the people in San Antonio could hear it. He wanted them to know that the Texans still held the Alamo.

INDEPENDENCE FOR TEXAS

The fighting at the Alamo was still raging when other Texans met to decide their future. They declared independence and soon chose David Burnet to be president. Sam Houston was put in charge of the Texas Army.

Houston only had a few hundred soldiers. Santa Anna had lost 1,500 men at the Alamo, but he still had thousands left. They marched to attack the Texans. Houston's army had to retreat.

For a month, the Mexicans chased the Texans. Every day, Houston's army grew stronger. Other Americans heard of the Texans' fight for independence and volunteers came to help, enlarging the force to 800 soldiers.

The Texans attacked the Mexican Army, shouting, "Remember, the Alamo!" In eighteen minutes, half the Mexicans were killed. Santa Anna was captured and forced to sign a treaty that gave Texas its freedom.

Fighting words

From the diary kept by Davy Crockett at the Alamo:
"We are all in high spirits, though we are rather short of provisions [food supplies], for men who have appetites that could digest anything but oppression: but no matter, we have a prospect of soon getting our bellies full of fighting, and that is victuals [food] and drink to a true patriot any day."

Texas gets its nickname "the Lone Star state" from its state flag.

WAR WITH MEXICO

In 1836 Texas became independent and was nicknamed the Lone Star Republic. The Texas government asked Congress to make Texas part of the United States. At first, Congress refused, but in 1845 Texas was admitted and became a state. This led to war with Mexico.

For ten years, Texas and Mexico had argued about the border between them. When Texas became a state, Mexican troops were sent to the Rio Grande, where they attacked a U.S. patrol and killed some soldiers. Congress declared war on Mexico.

U.S. soldiers invaded Mexico from two directions. One army marched south from Texas. Another force landed at Vera Cruz on the Gulf of Mexico and moved toward Mexico City. The Mexican army was larger, but the U.S. troops were better trained. The Mexicans were defeated and the war ended in 1848 with the Treaty of Guadalupe-Hildago.

In this treaty, Mexico had to recognize that Texas was part of the United States and give up more than 500,000 square miles (1.3 million square kilometers) of land.

MANIFEST DESTINY

The battle at the Alamo is an example of the fighting spirit of Americans at the time. People believed that the United States had a special purpose. The future president James Buchanan described this purpose as a mission "to extend the blessings of Christianity and religious liberty over the whole continent." This belief, that Americans were chosen by God to rule the continent, was called Manifest Destiny.

Manifest Destiny was partly based on racist ideas. Some whites thought that their culture and ideas were best. They thought they had a right and a duty to conquer Native Americans so they could teach them the benefits of white, Christian civilization.

American Progress was painted by artist John Gast. It shows the Spirit of Manifest Destiny traveling west.

TRAILS WEST

Rugged explorers known as mountain men traveled alone, carrying all of their possessions on their backs. They lived off the land and trapped animals for their fur. When mountain men came back to civilized areas to sell their furs, they told stories about new places and the best trails to use to reach them.

Other people followed the paths blazed by the mountain men. The best routes to the West became well-known trails. A few **missionaries** and settlers started using these trails in the 1830s. By the 1840s, thousands of people were migrating west across the Great Plains, grasslands that stretched from the Mississippi River to the Rocky Mountains.

Life on the trails was dangerous. Travelers faced rough land, harsh weather, and Native American attacks. Pioneers formed groups that worked together to survive the hardships. Most settlers had wagons, so the groups were called wagon trains. Before their journey started, wagon train members agreed on rules and elected a wagon master to lead them.

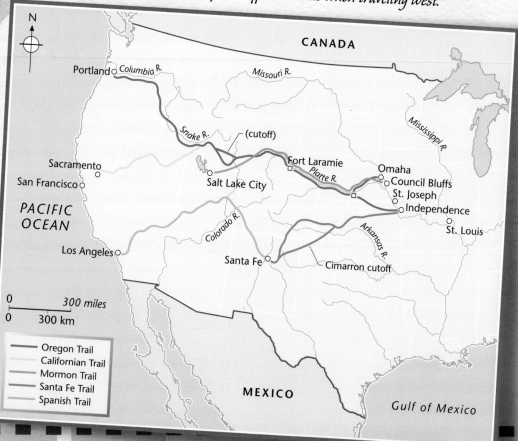

Settlers could choose from different trails when traveling west.

STARTING POINT

Many wagon trains were formed near Independence, Missouri. Settlers gathered in St. Louis and then rode a steamboat up the Missouri River to Independence. There, people purchased and organized wagons and supplies.

A conestoga wagon was a large, heavy wagon with beds in it. Its floor sloped, so the contents would not roll around.

Supplies for the journey

Pioneers packed their wagons with everything they would need to travel the trails and to establish new homes at their destinations. Most carried supplies and equipment that included flour, sugar, salt, bacon, coffee, tea, cornmeal, dried beans, pots and dishes, clothing, tools for repairing the wagon and building a house, and seeds and equipment for farming. Some also brought along a treasured piece of furniture or a few books.

THE SANTA FE TRAIL

The oldest of the routes from Missouri into the West was the Santa Fe Trail. William Becknell discovered it when he and four other men left Franklin, Missouri, on September 1, 1821, and headed west. The men rode horses and led pack mules loaded with goods. Becknell was a trader and hoped to swap the goods for horses, which would bring a good price back in Missouri.

The trading party traveled across Missouri, then Kansas, and followed the Arkansas River into Colorado. Becknell led his men southwest into the rough country. The men had to chop a trail through dense woods and move piles of rocks that blocked their way. They found a mountain pass that led them into New Mexico, which was Mexican Territory.

Some Mexican soldiers convinced Becknell to go to Santa Fe and trade his goods with the people there. The Mexican settlers in Santa Fe were eager to trade, and the men made a huge profit. They returned to Missouri already making plans for another trip.

The Santa Fe Trail crosses mountains and plains.

THE CIMARRON CUTOFF

On his next trip, William Becknell used three wagons so that he could carry more goods. He knew the wagons could not get past the boulders on the rough part of the trail, so they tried a different route. The men crossed the Arkansas River and traveled south across a desert to the Cimarron River. They almost died from thirst while crossing the desert, but finally made it to Santa Fe. Becknell sold his goods and returned to Missouri with a fortune.

When people saw that money was to be made by trading in New Mexico, many began to use the Santa Fe Trail. Most braved the desert route, called the Cimarron Cutoff.

Settlers joined the traders on the Santa Fe Trail. Some took the Cimarron Cutoff through the desert, while others traveled the rough trail.

Other trails

The trails were improved and eventually reached beyond Santa Fe. The California Cutoff led northwest into Utah. There, it became the Old Spanish Trail, which went all the way to California.

THE OREGON TRAIL

The Oregon Trail was the longest of the trails west, reaching more than 2,000 miles (3,200 kilometers) from Missouri to Fort Vancouver in present-day Washington. Lewis and Clark were the first white men to use parts of this trail on their expedition in 1804. They reported that the Northwest had rivers and streams full of beavers, otters, and other fur-bearing animals.

Fur trappers and traders heard the news and soon moved into the area. In 1808 John Astor, a New York City fur merchant, started the American Fur Company. He established a string of trading posts in the Northwest that were very successful. By 1834 his business was the wealthiest company in the United States. The fur traders and early missionaries sent back glowing reports describing Oregon's rich land. One said, "As far as its producing qualities are concerned, Oregon cannot be outdone."

Eagle Rock was an important landmark for travelers on the Oregon Trail.

TRAVELING THE TRAIL

People living in the East read reports of Oregon's rich land with great interest. Farmers dreamed of claiming a bit of fertile land on this new frontier. Many sold all of their possessions, packed up their families, and headed out. The Oregon Trail became the most used route to the West, with 350,000 travelers between 1840 and 1869.

The six-month wagon trip on the Oregon Trail was the most dangerous and difficult of all the wilderness crossings. This journey across half a continent took travelers over wild and varied landscapes, from hot deserts to freezing snow banks. They had to cross rivers and struggle up backbreaking mountains. Pioneers faced bad weather, diseases, food shortages, and the threat of Native American attack. Amazingly, most people survived the journey.

This is a building called Old Bedlam at the Fort Laramie National Historic Site.

Rest stops

Fort Laramie and Fort Kearny were located along the Oregon Trail. Travelers could stop at these outposts for repairs or supplies. On one day, June 17, 1850, the records at Fort Laramie show that 6,034 people passed by.

THE MORMON TRAIL

One large group of settlers came west for religious reasons. The Mormon Church started in New York in 1830, and from the beginning their beliefs brought **criticism** from other Christians. The Mormons were forced to move to Ohio and then to Missouri.

After being attacked by mobs in Missouri, the Mormons moved on to Illinois and finally decided to migrate west. They made a new route that came to be called the Mormon Trail. It led them to land where they founded a settlement that became Salt Lake City, Utah.

This is one of the first cabins built by settlers in the Great Salt Lake Valley.

WALKING THE TRAIL

Daily life in a wagon train was very tiring. Almost everyone had to walk. The only people who rode in the wagons were young children, the sick, and the elderly. The injured also rode, as ten-year-old Mary Ackley wrote:

My two brothers were playing in the wagon . . . the wheels went down in a rut which jarred the wagon, throwing brother John out. A hind wheel ran over him, breaking one of his legs . . . [He] was confined to the wagon for the rest of the long journey.

Some sections of the trail were littered with abandoned possessions. In a letter, Narcissa Whitman wrote:

Dear Harriet,
The little trunk you gave me has come so far & now I must leave it here alone. The hills are so steep [and] rocky that Husband thought it best to lighten the wagon as much as possible.

Plains Native Americans

To Plains Native Americans, the buffalo was their source of life. They hunted the large herds that roamed across the Great Plains. Native Americans used every part of each buffalo that they killed. They ate the meat and used the hides (skins) to make their homes and clothing. They made tools from buffalo bones and horns. Plains Native Americans lived this way for thousand of years before the settlers came.

This Mormon family stopped for a rest near Calls Fort, Utah, in 1867.

GOLD RUSH

James Marshall was a carpenter building a sawmill in California for Johann Sutter. One morning he spotted something shiny in the stream that flowed past the mill and bent over for a closer look. It was gold.

When gold was discovered at Sutter's Mill, the news spread like wildfire. Newspapers and magazines across the country printed stories about the fabulous wealth being dug from the ground in California. Not everyone believed the reports, but some did and immediately set out for the west coast. More people looking for gold meant that more gold was found and more stories were published. Hopeful **prospectors** by the thousands set out for California. The Gold Rush was on!

Gold!!

From a news story in the San Francisco *Californian* on May 29, 1848: "The whole country, from San Francisco to Los Angeles and from the seashore to the base of the Sierra Nevada, resounds with the sordid cry of "gold!! GOLD!!!" while the field is left half planted, the house half built, and everything neglected but the manufacturers of shovels and pickaxes."

The discovery of gold at Sutter's Mill began the biggest gold rush in history.

PROSPECTORS

People flocked to California from all over the United States and from Europe, South America, Asia, and Australia. Within a year, 100,000 newcomers had transformed California from a quiet land with few people into a frenzy of activity. A letter from a man in California that was printed in a Washington, D.C., newspaper described it this way: "At present the people are running over the country and picking gold out of the earth here and there, just as a thousand hogs let loose in a forest."

California or bust

Getting to California from the eastern states was dangerous. A traveler could take a ship down around the stormy tip of South America and back up the Pacific coast. Or he could sail only as far as Panama, march through a disease-infested jungle, and get on a ship heading north. Most chose to join wagon trains on land and brave Native Americans, rivers, and mountains.

Many people traveled to San Francisco on their way to the gold fields.

WESTERN GROWTH

The discovery of gold started years of rapid expansion in the West. Before the gold rush, only about 6,000 Mexican settlers and 500 Americans lived in California, plus thousands of Native Americans. San Francisco alone grew from about 400 Americans in 1845 to 35,000 in 1850. By 1852 the population of California was 250,000.

Most prospectors did not get rich, but merchants, factories, and freight companies made fortunes by supplying the needs of the miners. Many people who failed to find gold stayed on and became farmers or started successful new businesses. The burst of economic activity attracted even more settlers to the Pacific coast.

This buildup in the West caused some people to move back to the East. Up until this time, the region from the Mississippi River to the west coast had been considered a harsh, useless land. People had crossed it as quickly as possible and had not settled there. Now, led by prospectors who found fortunes in Colorado and Nevada, people moved east and began settling in previously empty areas. This led to new conflicts with Native Americans.

Mining towns popped up quickly after gold or silver was discovered nearby.

MORE FIGHTING

Traders and prospectors had not been bothered much while crossing Native American lands because they were just passing through. But when settlers moved in, building farms and killing buffalo, the Native Americans became angry and attacked the invaders. The violence between Native Americans and settlers continued for decades, but the settlers kept coming.

U.S. borders

To the north, the boundary between the United States and Canada was set by an agreement with Great Britain in 1846. The southern border of the U.S. was formed when a huge tract of land called the Gadsden Purchase was acquired from Mexico. The United States then reached from Canada to Mexico and from the Atlantic Ocean to the Pacific Ocean.

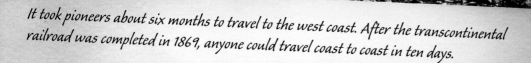

It took pioneers about six months to travel to the west coast. After the transcontinental railroad was completed in 1869, anyone could travel coast to coast in ten days.

SEA TO SHINING SEA

The completion of the Transcontinental Railroad was the end of the frontier. A cross-country trip that was previously long and hard was now quick and easy.

In less than a century, the greatest migration in history was completed. The rapid population growth and waves of immigrants created a flood of settlers, each seeking a piece of land. Their push west moved the border of the United States all the way to the Pacific Ocean.

By the end of the 1800s, the mass westward migration was completed and the nation had its basic shape. The conquest of the wilderness was a great achievement by the pioneers, and their country reached from sea to shining sea.

New commerce

Industry also expanded rapidly in the 1800s as the Industrial Revolution began. New machines and methods helped businesses to thrive. In 1820 less than 100 steamboats carried freight and passengers up and down rivers. By 1860 there were more than 1,000. New inventions like the reaper and the cotton gin made farming faster and easier.

As a result of the Industrial Revolution, factories and mills turned out more new products.

GROWING PAINS

Violence between settlers and Native Americans was terrible, but fighting was not the leading cause of death for either side. Native Americans killed about 7,000 settlers. In contrast, more than 30,000 pioneers died from disease while traveling the trails west. Thousands more did not survive their first winter in the wilderness.

Whites killed about 4,000 Native Americans in fighting. But new diseases brought by the settlers caused the deaths of millions. Some tribes were wiped out completely, and most lost more than three out of every four people. A Cherokee chief lamented, "Whole nations have melted away like balls of snow before the sun."

Native Americans have tried to keep many of their old traditions.

UNITED STATES MAPS

In just 100 years, the United States changed dramatically. These maps show how the nation grew between 1800 and 1900.

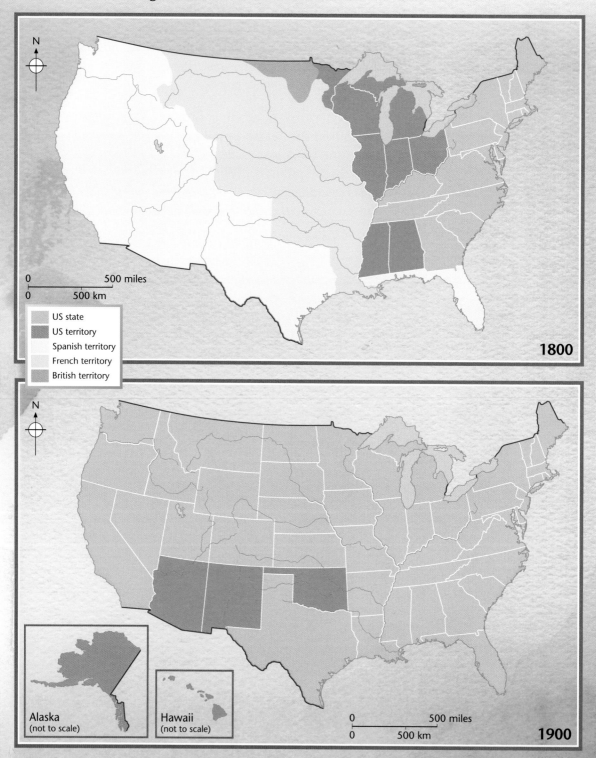

N

0   500 miles
0   500 km

US state
US territory
Spanish territory
French territory
British territory

1800

N

Alaska
(not to scale)

Hawaii
(not to scale)

0   500 miles
0   500 km

1900

TIMELINE

1803 France agrees to sell all of Louisiana to the United States for $15 million.
Meriwether Lewis and William Clark prepare for their expedition along the Missouri River to the Pacific Ocean.

1804 Lewis and Clark start their expedition.

1805 Lewis and Clark reach the Pacific Ocean.

1806 The Lewis and Clark expedition returns to St. Louis.

1808 John Astor starts the American Fur Company and establishes a string of trading posts in the Northwest.

1810 United States annexes west Florida (Alabama, Louisiana, and Mississippi).

1812 The United States and Great Britain begin the War of 1812.

1814 Treaty of Ghent is signed to officially end the War of 1812.

1815 The War of 1812 ends after the Battle of New Orleans.

1821 William Becknell creates the Santa Fe Trail. The first U.S. settlers reach Texas.

1828 Andrew Jackson elected president.

1830 Congress passes Indian Removal Act.

1836 The Mexican Army defeats Texans at the Battle of the Alamo. Texas battles the Mexican Army and wins. Texas becomes independent.

1838 Cherokees travel west on the Trail of Tears.

1845 Texas becomes a state. War with Mexico begins.

1846 The Mormons leave Illinois for Utah. The Mexican-American War begins.

1847 U.S. forces capture Mexico City and win war.

1848 Gold is discovered in California. Mexico and United States sign Treaty of Guadalupe-Hidalgo. United States annexes Oregon Territory.

1853 United States makes Gadsden Purchase from Mexico.

1869 Completion of the Transcontinental Railroad.

GLOSSARY

ally person or country working with another for a common goal, such as defeating an enemy

barrier something that stops people getting past

border dividing line between one country or region and another

cargo things carried by a ship or airplane

cede to give up power or land

colonist someone who lives in a newly settled area

colony land not connected to a nation, yet owned and controlled by it

Congress part of the U.S. government that makes the country's laws

constitution system of laws in a country that state the rights of the people and the powers of the government

criticism disapproval of what someone says or does

democracy form of government in which citizens make political decisions as a group, or elect others to make those decisions

discrimination mistreatment of someone because of a group he or she belongs to

expedition trip to taken for a specific reason, such as to explore unknown lands; also, the people who take such a trip

explorer one who travels to discover what a place is like

fort building that is strongly built to withstand or survive attacks

frontier largely unsettled border areas of a region or colony

governor person elected or appointed to control a political unit

immigrant someone who comes from abroad to live in a country

independence freedom from another person's or country's control

migration act of moving from one country or region to another

mission church or other place where missionaries live or work

missionary someone who is sent by a church or religious group to teach that group's faith or to do good works

natural resource material found in nature that is necessary or useful to people

Northwest Territory area that included all the land of the United States west of Pennsylvania and northwest of the Ohio River

orphan child whose parents are both dead

pioneer first person to do something, especially to settle in a particular region

plantation large farm where crops such as coffee, tea, rubber, or cotton are grown

policy general plan that people use to help them make decisions or take action

prospector person who explores or searches for something, like gold or silver

prosperous doing well, especially by making money

racist someone who thinks that a particular race is better than others or treats people unfairly or cruelly because of their race

route course that is followed from one place to another

settlement colony or group of people who have left one place to make a home in another

settler person who moves from one place into a new region

slave person forced to do work

syllable unit of sound in a word

territory area of land

treaty written agreement between two or more countries or groups

tribe group of people who share the same ancestors, customs, and laws

FURTHER READING

BOOKS

Isaacs, Sally Senzell. *The Oregon Trail*. Chicago: Heinemann Library, 2004.

Isaacs, Sally Senzell. *Stagecoaches and the Pony Express*. Chicago: Heinemann Library, 2004.

Isaacs, Sally Senzell. *The Trail of Tears*. Chicago: Heinemann Library, 2004.

Long, Cathryn J. *Westward Expansion*. San Diego, Calif.: Kidhaven, 2003.

Roop, Peter and Connie. *The California Gold Rush*. New York: Scholastic, 2002.

Steele, Christy. *Pioneer Life in the American West*. Milwaukee: World Almanac Library, 2005.

Stefoff, Rebecca. *The Opening of the West*. New York: Benchmark/Marshall Cavendish, 2003.

Wadsworth, Ginger. *Words West: Voices of Young Pioneers*. New York: Clarion, 2003.

INTERNET

Digital History: Learn About Westward Expansion
http://www.digitalhistory.uh.edu/modules/westward/

Native American Removal 1814–1858
http://www.pbs.org/wgbh/aia/part4/4p2959.html

The National Road
http://www.nps.gov/fone/natlroad.htm

The Oregon Trail
http://www.isu.edu/~trinmich/Oregontrail.html

The Trail of Tears
http://www.rosecity.net/tears

HISTORIC PLACES TO VISIT

The Alamo
955 S. Alamo
San Antonio, Texas 78299
Visitor Information: 210-225-7363

Museum of Westward Expansion
Jefferson National Expansion Memorial
11 North 4th Street
St. Louis, Missouri 63102
Visitor Information: 314-655-1700

Disclaimer
All the Internet addresses (URLs) given in this book were valid at the time of going to press. However, due to the dynamic nature of the Internet, some addresses may have changed, or sites may have changed or ceased to exist since publication. While the author and Publishers regret any inconvenience this may cause readers, no responsibility for any such changes can be accepted by either the author or the Publishers.

INDEX